S0-BBD-413

editor John F. Deane

CHICAGO PUBLIC LIBRARY
BEVERLY BRANCH
1962 W. 95th STREET
CHICAGO, IL   60643

Also by Macdara Woods:

Poetry:
"Decimal D. Sec. drinks in a Bar in Marrakesh", *New Writers' Press*, 1970.
"Early Morning Matins", *Gallery Press*, 1972.
"Stopping The Lights in Ranelagh", *Dedalus*, 1987.
"Miz Moon", *Dedalus*, 1988.

Translation:
"The King of the Dead and Other Libyan Tales" (with the author Redwan Abushwesha), *Martin Brian & O'Keefe*, 1978.

R07125 99981

" The Hanged Man
Was Not Surrendering "

by

Macdara Woods

DEDALUS

The Dedalus Press
24 The Heath, Cypress Downs, Dublin 6W, Ireland.

© Macdara Woods 1990

ISBN 0 948268 64 6 (Paper)
ISBN 0 948268 65 4 (Bound)

Cover Design: Graphiconies.

Printed by: The Nationalist, Carlow.

Acknowledgements are made to the editors of *Ambit* (London), *Broadsheet* (Limerick), *Cyphers*, *Orbis* (Nuneaton, England), *Poetry Ireland Review*, *Quarry* (Canada).

My thanks to Bernard and Mary Loughlin, and to Doreen Burns, Ingrid Adams and Ann McGuirk, of the Tyrone Guthrie Centre at Annaghmakerrig, where many of these poems were written.

The Dedalus Press receives financial assistance
from An Chomhairle Ealaíon, the Arts Council, Ireland.

No one was shot in Tiananmen Square.
　　　Peking Statement on the events of June 1989.

No one has seen a griffin.
Origen, in the fourth century AD, commenting on Leviticus xi. 13.

The heretic lies. I have seen a griffin.
　　　Ninth century Byzantine scribe, commenting on Origen.

The bloody massacre in Bangladesh quickly covered over the memory of the Russian invasion of Czechoslovakia, the assassination of Allende drowned out the groans of Bangladesh, the war in the Sinai Desert made people forget Allende, the Cambodian massacre made people forget Sinai, and so on and so forth until ultimately everyone lets everything be forgotten.
　　　Milan Kundera. The Book of Laughter and Forgetting.

Can I move? I'm better when I move.
　　　Butch Cassidy and the Sundance Kid.

CONTENTS

Scenes from the Compartment

Poems for a Wraith

Tavernelle

For Niall
six and swimming —
and like the rest of us
on loan from himself

and in memory of
his godfather —
Vivian Mercier 1919-1989

SCENES FROM THE COMPARTMENT

WORDS FROM A ONE WAY TICKET

I came abreast of my forty-sixth year Captain
since last I saw you —
nine hours out of Paris on the Napoli Express
six of us at five-twenty-five A M
stretched out in our couchette
on the wings of triplanes
wrapped in disposable fabrics
we are hot cryonics in a honeycomb
lifting up on the occasional elbow
to angle for the dawn —
and missing it at Torino Porto Nuovo
the cormorants bobbed awake at Genova
put on their daytime faces for La Spezia
where I fell down a marble staircase once —
But no stopping this time Captain
we will go beneath the hills past Pisa
in Florence maybe have a cup of coffee
and make my through connection for Terontola

Always hopeful of the great adventure
I listen to their heartbeats and survey the years
noting how we submerge like submarines
to surface maybe a decade later
when we are travelling down some Autostrada
and the rhythm sets a train of thought in motion
until late in the hazy afternoon
poised and quick on some foreign cross-roads
or striding some railway platform
you meet yourself
and learn that you are someone else
that all these years you have been someone else —
a civil servant in Salamanca
with a wife and child and mistress —
who sits too long over drinks in the evening
in some shadowed sandstone square playing dice

But while he survives I am moving into
another kind of bandit country
to learn what happens after forty-five:

The trees were bare when we arrived
it was thundery and cold
the kind of weather you imagine did for Shelley
and we burned off-cut logs from the mill
but now on this last day of April
I can see clear across the Plain of Umbria
and the clusters of houses dotted on the hill-tops
bear witness to the sympathy of stone —
no colour here seems out of place
where everything that is has rein to riot —
There is order in the frenzy of the light
all along the slopes beneath this terrace
I see the ranked descent of vines and olives
Figures of Etruscan Geometry:

And Captain — when I consider it
what else could I have done but travel on?
Is that not all there is?
Yet for the moment now I take a pause
naked on this Italian roof
under Monte Subasio to make an act of faith
drinking black tobacco in the sun

Agello 30-4-198

THE EGYPTIAN SINGER

That's all very well I said
to the painted angel on the festoon blind
that's all very well but
there's no love here no sensual heat
or none that I can make out
She threw her head back
clicked her fingers — What?
No love here? Don't be ridiculous —
she paused — on the other hand
it depends on what you want I suppose

There is a man outside my window
lithe as a cat
picking magic mushrooms
walking like a cat on the wet grass
caught up in his concentration
I have been watching him for hours
and for some time I thought he was picking worms
it is all so distant
picking worms or mushrooms
it depends on what you want I suppose

That Egyptian singer in the background
I listened to her when I was drunk
night after night with my hair matted
falling down the stairs
or staggering up to bed
and now I sit here
in a cone of hard white light
while she sings of love and sex and loneliness
it depends on what you want I suppose

ROCKPOOLS

1.
The distance of the glass ordains
the angles between stars and eyes
so looking deep into the mirror pool
she saw light years away
the flickering dog-star and the plough
And now it's little she remembers
her tearstained airmail letter to Paris
where fountains take the place of pools
and drunkenly I sang the Mass
and meant it too with someone else
The substance in the glass ordains
the character of chance or change

2.
The pen in my hand encumbers
both instinct and thought
confuses for a moment craft and numbers
and the white page — wilful as wind
remains the landscape of the albatross
mountainous blank unmarked

But gulls riding on an updraft
make flying look easy
past cliff-ledge and spindrift
ocean and sea-spray
innocent of sepia cuttle-fish ink
unaware of the quills in their wings

3.
In the aspen-leaved morning
he walks and thinks of lakes
lakes caught upon the summits of mountains
lakes green with islands
or blue with hard fish — plantings
cold hard and bare are the woods
in the aspen-leaved morning in winter

STREET SCENES: FEBRUARY 17th 1987

1.

A large backside camouflaged in a telephone kiosk
a self-help group flashes by in an Ambulance

& Roisín

eating sticky buns in the front seat of a car
cradling a sink-unit

2.

Driving past the Jesuits at night
I hear the ghosts of women in the Milltown Flats

3.

Cold bright northern weather
parents are getting frisky at the school gates
Election posters have bloomed around the lamp-posts

4.

All this is Yuppy Country
says the PD activist:
God doesn't play dice and McDowell gets in

5.

But at the corner of Aston Place and Bedford Lane
I read:

     Yobbo & Kosh
     Auds & Tomo
     Lorna & Martin
     Lisa & Stud

in white paint more permanent than print

MAKING AMENDS TO SUSA

When next you go to Susa
enquire for shade in the cavernous rooms
of the Hotel del Sole Susa
five beds to a room and you pay by the beds you use
in Susa

Mother-In-Law's Milk on sale in Susa
Mullingar voices in the piazza
electronic broom-sticks
and the parocco on the scaffolding viewing his roof
in Susa

All things come to Susa
the Teutonic Knights sweep in on motor-cycles
'In the compression-chamber of my heart . . .'
says the leader taking off his helmet
'A spark ignites for Susa'

And if I should ever run off again
it won't be with a red-haired woman to Ringsend
but with a strait-laced German baroness in Susa
to make disciplined sexual love in Susa
and take the air of an evening about the Augustan Arch

Alpine Susa
starting point of Italian Unification
I called you a rip-off joint in 1978
well . . . like all frontier towns
— and what a frontier the sharp Italian Frontier —
you are a joint and you rip people off

but a rip-off joint you are not

AFTER THE SLANE CONCERT: BASTILLE DAY 1987

The dark girl drinking cider in the bar
smiles speaking of her knife
my ears prick at the hint of violence
with thoughts of a dark street in Paris
almost thirty years ago
stoned high and fighting with a one-eyed Arab
above that Metro shelter
the quick flash of violence and sex
and short knives stabbing across the street

He was pissing sideways says the girl
like he wasn't aiming straight
and . . . and here her voice drops out of sight
her hair mingles with her neighbour's
like curtains falling across the street
I think of Borges' Argentinians
dying in limelight under street lamps
it is all so casual so promiscuous
so soft these lethal beautiful parishioners

And was it really just like this —
an inner city pub where careless Fates
blast on cider and cigarettes
so sure footed and so self-contained
that dangerous smile as innocent of violence
as the knife-blade in its hidden place
and one maimed look is all it needs
to make us human
reading in the morning ash for messages of love

SANTA MARIA NOVELLA

This lonely angular man in railway stations
going home by cloud or wherever and travelling collapso
in the polish of Santa Maria Novella
drinking an orange juice and smoking a gauloise
he pauses mid-journey poised and folded at his table
warily by times and almost paternal
he eyes his Gucci-type metal executive briefcase
his sorcerer's link with home and substance
as if he has just been told it contains a time bomb
and his time has ticked its hour up

Nor is he any too sure of these foreign coins
and he lays them out on his palm at intervals
to inspect them and survey them into sense
and all unbeknownst to him his eyebrows creep up
his head twitches to the side and his eyes widen
as he talks to the coins giving them instruction
and his other angular hand unships itself
an admonitory digit wagging up and down
until it anchors in under his chin
and he returns to the station self-service Ristorante
wondering if we have noticed his temporary absence

But we are all at odds here quartered off
set apart behind a bright green rope

I am considering the kilo of garlic in my bag
its oils and its fine rich weight and aroma
and this Florentine heat and I'm wondering
if my fellow passengers on the night train to Paris
will appreciate my addition to their journey
and all unbeknownst to myself
I have lifted the plastic bag to my head inhaling
as if to clear a lifetime of asthma
bursting my lungs with the must of garlic
I am tunnelling beneath the platforms of Florence
fiercely with my eyes shut
crushing wild garlic on the walls of my sett

Among the reflections and marble of Santa Maria Novella
magic samurai are sheathing magic cameras
a waiter slides by on velvet skates
an elderly German hitches up his shorts
the cool service area pauses unexpectantly
— again nothing has happened —
and the catch of the station clock flips over

SECONDS OUT

After Humpty Dumpty fell apart
they said they would reconstitute him
in the Tat Factory
iron out the folds in his carapace
rebuild him with sellotape and cowgum
three square meals a day
and some confrontation therapy

It would be hard they said
a stiff course for an egg
— an egg who suspected he'd be better off
robbing mail trains
or turning tricks on the canal bank —
a stiff course for an egg
but they would make a man of him

As in the end they did
a man of weights and measures
stripping five thousand crocus flowers
to procure an ounce of saffron:
in Cambodia there is no more gamboge yellow
and at the speed of light
sons are older than their space-men fathers

IN THE RANELAGH GARDENS: EASTER SATURDAY 1988

Easter falls early this year
at the end of a mild winter —
tomorrow the sun will dance on the ceiling
at midnight on Thursday by the sea I heard
Summer rustling in the palms

Listen said the voice
for years I have been fighting my way up out of this
climbing out of this black hole
pushing past the bog oak
and this black weight that hugs my rib cage

On a street corner in Rome my brother-in-law
the Guardian of Paradise reflects
Arabian gentleman in camel hair
how can I have grown so old he says
staring into his daughter's camera lens

I thought of him again last night
and looked for design in our ad hoc lives
breathing cool air from the surface of the pond
remembering I must not be in competition
not even with myself

Listen said the voice
for years I have been in the shallows of this lake
a creature of the reeds
hunting under drowned and folded leaves
with the water beetles

ANGELICA SAVED BY RUGGIERO

This girl I recognise her
from the filleting room at the back of Keegan's
dismembering North Sea haddock saithe and spur-dog
now at nine o'clock in the morning
I watch her striding through the dry-ice air
red hair the colour of insides of sea-urchins
herself like an underwater creature
she flits and darts through the morning traffic
wrapped around in her red and white stripes
to the shade and shell of her souk

I caught her in a net and brought her home one night
as befits me a convicted anarchist
who himself keeps a roadside stall in Tripoli
not far from the Azizia barracks
a thousand miles east of the Rue Bab Rob
one month's journey through the territory of ostriches
a two month journey travelling by ostrich
subsisting only on their chalky eggs

I seized her like a myth and brought her home
to this courtyard market and charnel shambles
my carpeted rooms up under the roof
sat her on the floor and to protect her from the night
wrapped her in a kefía from Damascus
gave her a gold-work kaftan and slippers for her feet
filled glasses of mahia from Marrakesh
served mejoun and mint tea on an inlay table
and coffee taken from the heat three times
thick black coffee from Cairo

And up beneath the slippery roof
we skewered fish kebabs and prawns for a feast
clams caught that morning in Essaouira
while we gazed out through the windows at the sky
past Rats' Castle and the old men's home
beyond the Burlington to the mouth of the river
suspended in the silver nitrate moon
and the minarets of the Pigeon House
until I saw her deep-sea eyes cloud up

This happens in mid-sentence
with our fingers on the page we lose our place
delaying we were caught between the tides
while the foreshore lengthened all around
into a dim anonymous suburban pub
with the elements and furniture of sea-wrack
rising up from the floor to claim us
ash-trays and razor-shells a palm-court pianist
and in the corner hung with sea-weed
a supermarket trolley rusting in the sand

The level sands stretched out and that was it
new myths spring up beneath each step we take
always another fact or proposition missed
and just for a moment we almost touched
though she knows nothing of it now in cold December
dancing out of the Ingres painting
and making her way down the morning street
she pauses in mid-stride then looks away
freed from that scenario of chain and rock
Andromeda — this girl — I recognise her

LINES READ AT THE UNVEILING OF A HEAD OF TYRONE GUTHRIE

Picture an ornamental garden
on the shoulder of the world in winter
with sundial and geometric pattern
fences to keep back the fields
and crows like musical annotations
in the hard wind blowing down the hill

Unmysterious space of garden
laid out in gravel paths and beds for figures
lost and found in the present tense
working or walking or welded to the spot
not on display in place yet lit
and inexplicable as items in a gallery

A whole Toledo city of perspectives
functional and unpretentious
tilting into the winter solstice —
mistakenly I have been trying to formalise
some step to take me out to join
the figures in the winter leaves

Until in time I am surprised in space —
as the ordinary will always be surprising
as this garden is surprising
or the back-lit cyclist on the road from Clones
fifth horseman on the hump back bridge
rearing out of the morning mist

Or the inhaler shapes along the avenue
mushroom houses breathing in the rain
anywhere and nowhere —
and when you come around the corner
the mediaeval landscape of McGorman's yard
is timeless as a cinquecento street

With time and space to be astonished
in this slanting Northern light —
packing up to move along again I know
that when I'm beating down the road to Dublin
there will be more going on
than cheap petrol and the BBC Third Programme

Annaghmakerrig 12-11-1988

MAN ON THE DOORSTEP

He knocks on my door at night
the howling storm made visible
raves at me like conscience
come out he says come out
come out and see the holes in the road
the holes in the road in the rain
it is all falling down around us
holes full of water for children to fall in
and he is right —
five minutes is all it would take
take five to walk to the bottom of the hill
to see these childrens' graves in the rain

But I can't go out
because I am minding a real live child
I am father to a child
who eats and sleeps and goes to school
flies kites and brings me paintings
and keeps his margins to the edge of the page
or as near as he can at five and a half
who is not for the moment homeless
and depends on me to keep the night outside

Tá Bran ar scoil
Tá Micí ag gáire Tá Lúlú ag gol

No you can't come out says the man
but you can go to bloody Umbria —
and what are you going to do about this
Fascist descent into Anarchism?
What are the artists of Ireland doing?

Safeguard your reputation

I was here this morning in this very place
in this very place today — and
he digs his heel into the crumbling pavement —
and I said to an Indian doctor
an Indian doctor from the College of Surgeons
how can people live in this
in this city falling apart
seeing this same shit day after day and every day
head shaking like John O Gaunt
this same shit and nothing else
enough said said the doctor —

Do you realise
that in the European Parliament
the whole of Europe is laughing at us?
The Germans are laughing at us
the Italians the French
the Greeks and Spaniards are laughing
laughing into their translation machines
laughing like drains
like the rain falling on Dublin they laugh
and the British shoot us

He moves away into the night —
Safeguard your reputation with Cess-Clean
says the advertisement on national radio

In the cafe window seat
looming in leather jacket
buckskins and bodywave
he sits up and says
it's the stupidest thing in the world you know
to point a gun at someone —
to point a gun at someone he nods
and not pull the trigger

Beside him enthuses
a wide-eyed breathless girl
oh it is oh it is oh it is
and just like that
they have it all worked out
here by the Perpetual Laundrette

And I am wondering
where I might find clean clothes —
really clean clothes
that smell of mountain flowers
carded and separated fibres
lighter than journies in sun and snow —
not stiff with age and guilt
and battered train trips
from Dublin to London London to Dublin
coloured by memories of Collis Browne
and weariness
and the killing fields at Crewe

A proud male transient
                    he stamps the plastic
spoons and knives into the floor —
Why do you live in a country
where it rains all the time?
And bitch about it?
It seldom drops past seventy in Mexico
and you can live on a dollar a day —
maybe more if you smoke cigarettes

From the corner:
Why do Americans come over here?

Beneath the table out of sight
of their companions
she lays her hand upon his thigh
little bird
it rivets me

Outlined against the inside of the window
with Merry Xmas and Christmas trees reversed
she extends a finger
and he moves upon it mouthing like a fish
licks her hand and sucks her cuticle

Gathering my coat about me
I rise to leave
thinking of a summer in Berkshire
sometimes sleeping rough
and on the morning after
watching a breathless wide-eyed girl
in a field drink Johnnie Walker

FELLOW PASSENGERS

Words come falling
from this silhouette
coiled up tight
with his back to the light
fragments of words —
twitching and dangerous

I see him blunted
reader of the Sun
bringing our boys back home
tatooed with blood and printed
on his left hand MICK
jerking in the undergrowth
deranged and dangerous

Some unequal force
smashed a bottle
in his skull at birth —
he reaches out
to stab his fingers in my face:
Can I have a
have a light then? Hey?

Bit of all
Bit of all right then?
Sits down his fingers
beating on the table top
takes up his friend and quest again:
The Jewman in James' Street
you know the poofter him

In and out job — quick
no hanging about
know what I mean? Are you on?
The beast is loose
persuasive now
he drops his eyes
his claws and tongue protrude

Him on the hill
he wheedles
him on the hill is King
is King — you know what I mean?
He wets his lips and whispers
It was after —

I was there my son
and it was after —
after sweet michelle
he done her in

THE BELLA FIGURA

Of a sudden in the afternoon
I found him
lurking motionless and purposeful
breath suspended
in the shade in my long front garden
a man from the pub
who is all mankind or was
Is he not my neighbour like the rest
even those who persecute and

It is not clear what he is at
red faced and caught off guard
he pretends to be staring at the wall
then strikes out accusingly
angrily — By God he says
By God but *you've* made a great recovery
A great recovery —
Do you know that?
I remember when no one could talk to you

That is enough now —
I shall die of that
Said Ferdia

Little Hound —
In one of these houses another neighbour
an elderly woman broke her hip last week
and treated the break with Wintergreen
treated the break for days with Wintergreen
In our arms we carried her
from bed to threshold
on the river-bank we laid her down
in the shelter of chariot wheels

Too well tempered by the ghosts
and vampires who walk up and down my stairs
clothed in memories of MIMS Directory
I am weary of ignorance
and still locked up —
still watching the prison weather cock
weary of ignorance
and tired of visitations

What incarnations in the garden
surprise — resentment
or reverberation of skulls beneath the hearthstone
mislead you to believe
that we are talking
that we have anything to say
that you are talking to me now?

LETTER FROM COLLE CALZOLARO

LETTER FROM COLLE CALZOLARO TO
LELAND BARDWELL

All this month of August
I have been walking to the top of the hill
between fields of sweet lucerne
looking at the road across the valley
twisting upwards like a swan's neck
through scattered houses and slopes of olive
to the Saint Sebastian in Panicale
and alone on my hillside
in a rocky space between two vineyards
I have been thinking of love and death
taking no shelter from the sun
burning back into the landscape
going back dying back
like the sunflowers on the hills beneath

Writing for the shadow of a wraith
in the first late August mist —
there is a touch of dying in the air tonight
the harvest moon comes up
on the left hand of the house
bears down upon the trees between us and the road
eleven shrouded pines
blood orange for the wolves tonight
and the white road up into the mountain
looks black enough for Spanish horses —
do you remember Cocteau's horses —
an empty place and road like that
a rocky neck of hillside
hard and bare and white with lunar dust

Soon it will be time to travel North again
leaving behind us
the outline of an imprint in cool water
a moving shadow at the bottom of the pool
vestigial boundaries marked
on Land Commission photocopy paper
or the undeveloped image left
when Niall looked into a well one night
at the Festa in a neighbouring town
and his reflection came leaping up the cistern
like a fish-child leaping from the sea
there was a woman at a window with a fan
and the band was playing Fior di Spagna
next year at the sign of St. John

This year next year of a mind to stay here
working — separating images
the August thunderstorms
and the August fireworks
the lamps of the combine harvesters
swallowing up the hills at night
and build a capanna on the hillside
dig in under a bamboo roof
leaving the rest of the action to the posse
those mock satires choreographed debates
chat show spontaneity where everything is planned
as the scripted confrontations
of the bo-peep personalities —
their breathless indignations

Not that I mind travelling North
travelling anywhere or travelling back —
those Autumn mornings in Hereford
in the hop-yards in the rain and mud
there was ice in the air
and the vines were not altogether different
the same patina of copper sulphate
but they were taller — sharper
something to wrestle with
wrenching them down from the wires
pulling them down by the armful
as they scored us across the mouth and eyes
marked us with pickers' scars
that had us refused in the Tory bars

The problem is clawing out space and time
all summer the house
has been full of children flies and guests
and in that dimension
between what is done and what is finished
little of what we set in motion is completed
voices come between me and the page
I see cosmetic work on bubbled plaster
screens against the mosquitoes
but no damp course as yet in place
and water not made good to drink —
and through it I am writing for this wraith
keeping faith with a myth
in a play which has not occurred as yet

Coming up to midnight in a low white room
taut with the sound of strings
I am putting together this note for you
another outlaw like myself
sending back news from the edge of things
and getting as little thanks for it —
why is it always like pulling teeth?
Thinking of how Louis Armstrong said it —
don't fuck with *my* hustle —
to a bandsman who turned up drunk
what dispensation did they claim
in the Saturday pages of the Irish Times
for cowboy subcontracting — to fuck up
ten years' work in half a dozen hasty lines

And then the warnings on isolation
I have have I not heard talk
been told to be thankful for what I've got
as I am — and still dissatisfied
and all this counsel on losing touch
begins to sound like a lunar joke
to a man on the moon these twenty years
since nineteen sixty-nine at least
and not at all sure how it came about —
those shoes I borrowed from Jack Walsh?
And yet we pass for normal in the street
no wires or flashing lights
or space-age gear to mark us out — more like
inhabiting the day and getting on with it

The hanged man's shadow falls across the page
in the Autumn Arcades
the windows of the shops are full
but I find no wares of mine displayed
no poems in the anthologies
not even in the Airport Bookshop
which is hard to credit after twenty-seven years
not good approaching the wind of fifty
beginning to notice the chill upon the vines
and the mist beneath the bedroom window
but for the moment not important
I am still light enough on my feet
still camped outside the gates of Moscow
and damned if I retreat

Not bravado or head down doggedness
still less a stoic up against the wall
just staying open to whatever comes
remaining faithful to a myth
and is this any more fantastical
than Dante writing of Beatrice
or the aged Ronsard in pursuit of love
straining after a Maid-in-Waiting
or running for a bus with the Maid of Erin
just arrived in Dublin from Detroit
or finding mutual absent friends
in Grafton Street with Archie Markham
for a moment putting geography in place
before the city turns inimical again

Keeping faith with destiny perhaps
which is seldom recognisable
there are so many Postes Restantes
so many kinds of faithlessness
staying abreast of the long white road
remaining open to the impetus
hoping to recognise the moment when it happens
in whatever form it comes
the dangerous invitation to the cornfield
or Olean to Buffalo with Thomas Merton
ginseng tea in the back of the car
oxygen tanks in the boot
the driver reciting slow down slow down
and the quiet pause in St Pacificus

Which leaves me here at the end of August
writing these poems for a wraith
stripped to the bone for sun or rain
with all my naked longing on display
and feeling more isolated
stone cold sober more alone than ever —
I could be gone like Robert MacBryde or John
what holds me back but that my heart is taken
broken for love of a summer child —
and this is true — and it has come to this
otherwise it is easy
Qasbah walls going back into the desert
going back dying back and myself
dying back like a root in the hillside

September 2nd 1989

POEMS FOR A WRAITH

LONG DAY SHORT NIGHT SHE DANCES

1.

Drums coalesce the beat steps up
and she dances out eyes down makeshift
she slides across the sandy floor
arms lifted like a child
little more than a child she is
the household's daughter
an endangered balancing act
juggler in the family group
Soho whiskies and her mother's brandies
reflect acryllically about her steps
shanghaied and hijacked by a myth
the legend of her father
she is too old now for the show — too old
to be tossed around like Buster Keaton
too young to be sawn in half like this —
a black ball rolls across the floor
as we remember it
she had been dancing thus for years

2.

On cue tonight the band strikes up
the floating platform band
his mouth a husk the singer struts
with bulging microphone in hand
he tries for geographical escapes

Take me down to the Shining City
the industrial chimneys and the lots
life is short and your lips are soft
take me down by the shore tonight
take me down by the river steps
on the seaward side of the railway tracks
take me out to Buenos Aires
my lady of the river mouth

It is the longest day of the year tonight
the sea is glutinous and quiet
with an orange moon above the mountains
night stops at the Hill of Howth
and fire-ships in the bay light up
the shrouded figures here
the lay-by flash of thigh and breast
these timeless isolated
lovers of the dark

3.
It is afternoon the town is shut
I am here in the sun in an open boat
holding a small black owl in my hand
I am a child
a woman leaning toward me leaning forward
ringed fingers glinting on the oars
backwards and forwards back and forth
giving me birth or swallowing me up
sculls us to an island
we are newly eloped from her mother's house
sailing across the bay to freedom
a back-parlour bar up against the cliff
filled with tackle and tack
the smell of leather and sherry wine
and sun and skin and innocence:
before the boat can reach the slip
the black owl drops from my hand
and falls to the swimmers far beneath
so many swimmers
so many countless pilot fish

21-6-1989

SHARING HOUSEROOM

At night you can see around the corner
in the mirror in the corridor
depths deeper than the lake
at the end of that tubular perspective
another hallway and a door
upon another landscape
a door with spring-action iron bolts
above the ascendent steps
the trim box-wood
and the elusive carriageway beneath —
So much for the Set:

On call
throughout the afternoon we wait
for mirror-spots to point our marks
and give us room to move —
the director sits behind a curtain
his pockets full of stones
with which to pelt the audience
— if indeed we have an audience —
playing Argentinian dance-music
and the air is sweet
with tobacco smoke and dust

The language will be silent
the language to be used
when finally he calls on us for action
language of an age
when invitations were spontaneous
the widening of the iris
sweat on the lip
quickening of body-heat
erectile hairs
swift familiar acrid scents
and in that invented place of taste and touch
there will be urgencies
and urgency will bring it off

In the meantime the house is ours
more or less —
full of scene-shifters and birds of passage
lighting-men and an undertaker
driving nails in the attic

And in the meantime carefully
alone behind our several doors
like absent friends we rehearse ourselves
plot fantasies
interpret our edgy symptoms
eat — sleep
parcel up sheets for the laundry
listening always for sounds of contact
footsteps in the room above
the creaking riser on the stairs
a cough or sob in the corridor
and waiting always always straining
for that quick catch of breath

DEATH IN VENICE: PANICALE, AUGUST 1989

You opened a gate in a field
for the hanged man to shamble out
after years of fencing —
and I thank you for the summons
will you dress me for the part?
What cover should I wear
to go back to Venice for the day
al fresco on the Lido
in the Strawberry Beds in the open air —
long beige woolen scarf
battered felt hat?
Smart tie and handkerchief
jewellery and scents —
von Aschenbach himself descending
the stairs to meet the Press?

It is important —
some time today in the afternoon
we play the death scene
maybe naked
or maybe you will wear a long Edwardian dress
Victorian elastic-sided boots
and the light of course will be perfect
under your wide-brimmed hat —
thus far it is a fantasy
flesh and blood but still a fantasy —
we are in a cornfield
alone together in the full scirocco
put here by the make-up man
with ice and wine
and water to keep down the dust

It is a fantasy
in a field we have not entered yet
some nameless lot past Chapelizod
I see you standing waving
turning from the waist up
one hand resting on your hip
beckoning and pointing
pointing to a Summer in Provence
with the Iles d'Hyères on the horizon
and we are both nineteen again
working on the vendange
penniless and truly burnt
working our way to the head of the field
and the water and wine and blocks of ice
in the shade in a wooden box

It is later now and tense
in this imaginary garden —
the strawberry vendor has been
with his basket of dead-ripe fruit
there is a cloud along the Lido and the river
children's voices in the cornfield
and women calling them back
Tadziu — the sound hangs in the trees
Tadziu Tadziu — the woman with the pearls
but we play out the fantasy
streaked with sweat and dust
diving coming up for air
recording each other's imprint
until night
and the light we know will be perfect

THE COUNTRY OF BLOOD-RED FLOWERS

Looking out the window
six hours since I heard the Angelus
and there is no heavenly music
in the air above the house

Waiting for the dancer
to arrive across the fields tonight
with bag and bandages — a black
silk blindfold for my eyes

The window is unbarred
for locked cells may not be opened
where we find ourselves
in the country of blood-red flowers

Red flowers that bloom
at random in the chambers of the brain
along the blood
and lock into the mind and heart

She waits and she is right
little coelacanth — serpent brother
out there in the forest undergrowth
I hear her hesitate

Looking for patterns
she reformulates her steps —
again to the light of our lost rooms
love brings its own contagion

THE MIRROR FISH

Too much alone
I am uneasy here —
this silver light selects
lights random images

One day in Vézelay
approaching through the fields
my head dizzy
it was hard to breathe
under the weight of the great stone roof
red tumbrils of Côte du Rhône —
at the curt stone foot
of that cascading cliff of stone
a sick bat trapped
at the base of a column
in a shaft of sunlight
crawled nakedly for shade
mouth open
head thrown back
small teeth small rictus lips

Abandon had I known it
in a nearby house
a woman I had lived with
was making love
behind an eighteenth century façade
in an eighteenth century bed
looking down upon the orchard
making love in French

Years after in my turn
after the reunification of Italy
I came to myself in an empty bed
with all that world
that Ancien Régime
gone over to the enemy
to find the bat returned
a wistful outstretched messenger
a hanging crucifix
small trapped childish face
hunched up — stapled by the sun
to the mosquito blind

Hanging drunk
hanging like a tipsy sailor
or a passenger in panic
on a ship going down
hanging in the rigging
head thrown back and to the side
transfixed —
Santa Maria della Vittoria
I knew a woman once in Vézelay
with that same rictus of the lips

The moon is up
and in this solitude and nightmare
nothing is resolved
I am a tarpon
moving unseen —
the large mirror of these scales
reflects the ocean
this sheet of water here beneath the moon —
this is not translucence

TIME AND THE ICE-FISH

This is it now the lighthouse
any further we can not
than the sea-wall's end
like the others we must drop back

This week-end — in a day or less
they are turning the clocks back
and we will hear the cogs mesh
and the minutes begin to tick

Because there is no respite
from the knowledge in the blood
this is a fearful country this
bleak landscape of the ice-fish

MIZ MOON

Just one time more Miz Moon
here by the lakeside waiting for the dark
testing out these inland moorings
milestones and mornings in fading rooms —
do you remember the rooms Moon?
The smell of rooms?

Dust after rain in Marrakesh
sweet smell
cummin and coriander blowing on the wind
cedar and cream and almonds
jus d'amandes
okra rosemary petrol-fumes and kif

Running before the wind Moon
every day down to this
museum of furniture and memories and rooms
all to be vacated before noon
I hook onto phrases pictures scents —
do you remember the Delfin Verde?

Or white mornings up in Azrou
temporary cool in the Rif
and the smell of cool crisp flowers in the Atlas —
our tiled hotel in Ouarzazate
a nestling cruciform scorpion
asleep under the arch of my boot

Patterns of grace notes —
the bat's wing stretched is a dusty leaf
there is no one now beneath the willow
but blue and vacant glaze
and on the stairs at night I smile for the camera
this time turned by a ghost

Looking down now like Peter Quint
I see two figures in a boat traverse the lake
laughter after movement
till distance takes them in among the trees
we inhabit rooms of pictures Moon
ceramic pictures: painted plates

Who is this Moon you ask
who is Miz Moon?
Like a trumpet blast in Còrdoba
Moon in the morning throws the shutters open
with a Chinese finger on your pulse
sensuous Moon is focussed

Moon is wild garlic
after forty years of determined self-destruction
of giving the bump and grind to time
she has time now only for the jugular
free of politesse or politics
urgent Moon is infamous

Infamous Moon
making a monstrous lizard of the road
screwed everyone she met until
the alkali desert south of Albacete
cool Moon riding — on a crate
of Carlsberg Special and an ounce of dope

Robbed Banks
became a figure on surveillance tape
took a Diploma in History —
affected a Nurse's uniform
to run Crimi's Venereal Clinic in Naples
until Doctor Crimi turned her out for drink

Went to pieces in Tortosa
from the bodyweight of alcohol and Crimi's pills
jumped from a balcony
and holding six broken ribs in place
retracing her shambling steps
drove non-stop from Barcelona to Le Havre

Missed the boat
and sank without a trace —
Her progress halted she is all of this and yet
which one is Moon?
I hear party sounds from Sunset Boulevard
and Von Stroheim in the garden breaking ice

Fearful of rejection
I am too quick to put the blame on Moon
her indecision and her machinations
those fantastic ill timed assignations
I wonder if she ever could speak straight
until I remember Moon herself is hurt

No better suited for rejection
she has seen too many years in bars
too many afternoons in bed
fighting with hangovers and sleeping sickness
she understands too well
that stump of flesh we carry round

And what have I in turn to bring to Moon
here and now domestic me
that I should take her sometime lover's place
keeping my hot eyes off her daughter
every old man jack of me?
He gave her a child and was good about the house

All day today I walked the house
and the outhouse buildings and the forest path
keeping my side of the tryst
keeping myself for Moon at last
no Moon and the double cross cuts deep
etched in my window by the dawn

And at this point Miz Moon herself
the real Miz Moon
steps from the door to the hall porter's desk
sound of the oud and Oum Khalsoum
signs her name with a curlew feather
oval-eyed innuendo Moon

Now Moon and I in our separate corners
are much like any other couple
I haul the luggage up
she pauses on the stairs to order breakfast
we kick the fading fire awake and sleep
untroubled by fidelities

With Moon in the Botanic Gardens
I stepped into a Chinese print
of figures hidden in among the leaves
saffron horsemen on a hill
a woman dancing with a fan
in pools of white behind the evergreens

By the oriental stream in Finglas
Moon rested for a time
beneath a variation of the willow
Moon spoke of Highland flowers
what I missed most up there she said
was the simple sound of birds

There was no birdsong on the crags
when Moon went walking on the Mongol border
athletic Moon on tour
climbed over tor and fell and scar
horned goat-Moon
kneeling at every crescent station

Restless Moon slips under glass
strolls drily through the beds of cacti
spread at her feet like kidney beans
thinks of Arizona and her travels in Peru
lakes and floating islands
and dipping stone-birds on the sea

In the moist air of the hothouse
tropical Moon at last alone
lay down among the roots of bamboos
listened to water dripping from the roof
sloughed off memories and skins
all through the humid afternoon

Moon dined with serpents
satyrs and hyenas coupled in the ferns
supported by a plinth of polished stone
Moon surveys the circus unamazed
disdainfully — a maja Moon
olympian hand in place Miz Moon reclines

Heigh-ho says Moon and what do I want
running away from home like this
taking refuge in the lake —
tangled up in images
turn turn to the wind and the rain
would they leave me be when the job is done?

Creaking down the stairs at night
with a bag of celibate laundry
she feels this is no way to spend a life
turning herself into a fantasy
a grown person should be more urgent
more troubled by realities

Understanding the market —
take a course in assertiveness
build mushroom cities and marinas
read and re-read the operators' handbook
and the cost-analysis of friendship
learn to push herself as product

Not turn her head into a voodoo hall
a Grand Guignol burlesque
smoking and going for healthy walks and smoking more
burning forty cigarettes a day
lying awake with pains in the chest
examining herself three times daily

And going outside to spit in private —
dear God says Moon
I have left my two precious lungs in shreds
all over this ornamental garden
I think I shall not be let out —
this white horse goes nowhere

Suddenly swaybacked with desire
Moon closed her eyes and shook her head
borrowed a bag and took time off
booked in for the nearest sea-port town
and slept all night by the harbour wall
with a heigh-ho the wind and the rain

One afternoon in sunlight Moon
lying on a hillside
as she thought safe among the plantings
saplings rising all around her
watched a stain of purple spreading on her arm
what fresh hell is this said Moon

No mort phthisique for Moon
despite what might be waiting in the script
she did not intend to start upon a slow decline
or some day sit silently at table
a superannuated mafiosa
shrouded against the light

Child of her generation
Moon would always be so blonde on blonde
death if it came for her would come
quick on a summer afternoon
when she was all sex and flesh and fruit
crushed ice and music

Time and genes decided else
and the wild rose grew back upon the stock
fire flashed along the hillside
Moon stared at the purple mark
the purple hair that sprouted from her breast
lake and sky flared suddenly and fierce

Sickened by light
Moon hid away in darkened rooms
watching the shadows of cats through windows
she walked the stone-flagged passages at night
noting the smell of age in the sheets
in a world of mirrors and books

Diehard Moon porphyric self-contained
she moved through all the phases of derangement
dressed in purple by appointment
turned the night to day and dreamed
of far-flung campfires and the glint
of red tinged fluorescent teeth

It was not an Aztec dream Moon
you put me in a matriarchal frieze
of women moving as planets move
across cold desert nights —
this woman's eyes devour this man
he stares down at himself in bloom

But a shadow has intruded
some tension grafted on the lovers here
hooked in position
allowed no momentary gesture of desire
I hear a rumour of resentment
reptilian politics

I look again at the Mexican colours
and think of Frida Kahlo —
here in the country of Madre de Dios
we learn our remorse from the waist down
if I use Moon she uses me
what else is there but leaning in to it

And leaning in without regret
the rest is a confusion
of maps and schemes and talk of soixante-huit
and who's design is this —
who marked out this frieze?
Is everyone reptilian in the end?

Hush child said Moon that will do you now
you have said your piece move on
we part again with no regrets
although in truth it has been hard enough
hard enough and I am hollowed out
weary as a stone

Today I watched a bird in flight
above the lake fall faultlessly
stall and fall wheel dip for bait
flying back upon the lake to retrace its path
dropping without regret
fly and stall falter fall and touch

fly stall falter fall and touch

TAVERNELLE

FIGS

I woke in panic in the heat
floating through the middle of the night
over the furnace of the pizzeria
not daring to turn on the light
for fear of bringing the mosquitoes in
or waking my son from sleep —

Christ that I could disentangle
just one dimension before the day comes back
working like that Gaelic bard in the womb of the boat
putting the bones of his poem in place —
Captain I am sleeping here below
below decks in the worm bitten rafters

I am putting memories in place
and calling-in on disused expertise —
the eel-net in the shed calls up but cannot save
energies spilled out on sand —
like the lost music of the Horn Concertos
vale come un fico secco

Dazed and isolated in the garden —
like this new fig-tree planted yesterday
a touch of acid green not much taller than my son
already fixing in the ritual stones
roots sunk in sand to keep them cool —
the day moves on and I am come adrift

To come to in Tavernelle —
we have made a shift to put our house in order
buying beds and hoisting home a fridge
putting a new hose on the butane cooker
having the water analysed
replacing broken windows

All these are basics and still I am adrift —
imprisoned in the evening shade
marked by time and that Sicilian cut
sometimes I feel the sun has failed me
squeezing out the years like juice
without even the choice of maize or sunflowers

We carry on because there is no choice
stung by times to anger and resentment but
without intercession still making a fist of it —
plastering the cracks with functional stucco
hacking at the same impenetrable thorns
hammering at the same blank pages

SCORPIONS

I built a castello of stones and mud
and great baulks of seasoned timber
with oak doors in the walls
and then I whitewashed the walls on the inside
put a fire-back and pots in the fire-place
a new-forged crane and hooks and chain
and in preparation for the siege ahead
I laid in logs and charcoal
onions and oil and garlic
and sides of bacon hanging from the beams
and then I sat back and waited
this whole peninsula was waiting
and I was European and waiting for the Barbarians

That German tonight in Castiglione del Lago
drunk lifted up a woman's dress
his companion night-jars screeching in the dark
pesca di mare pesca di mare
laughing their way up the cobbled street
pesca di mare pesche di mare
her curved gold abdomen a peach?
And in Panicale yesterday another
a madman torched himself and teenage son
we heard the ambulance climb screaming up the hill
the Corriere dell' Umbria in hot pursuit
and I thought of WeeGee
WeeGee flashing through the New York night
shadowing death for the Saturday Post
and I was European and waiting for the Barbarians

And in the end like dreams they came
black scorpions came down my walls to join me
finding recognition in the whites of my eyes
soot creatures from before my childhood
from that rain-streaked chimney space
black scorpions came down my white wash walls
and I know the limits of this farm-house hearth
what people occupied this place
my grandmother's bedroom stretching away
away from the house and the hill and the furze
my dead uncles standing like frozen horses
and the beasts that stamp and knock beneath
and I am European and waiting for the Barbarians

SUNFLOWERS

There was a moment I could have caught there
this afternoon on my steps
loose in the sunlight
seen fit to die here
looking down the hazy road toward Tavernelle
and the insects fluttering their day away
above my dusty sunflowers

There was a moment there I almost caught
when I recognised my father in myself
not the young man in photographs
foot on chair in revolutionary stance
but as I see him now
looking at me from the mirror
as I joke with my son about the motorcycle gobdaws
in the fields nearby
churning the red earth up

As I think we might have joked
reporting on the walkie-talkie
about the number of frogs in the irrigation ditch
since the coming of the water-snake
and gone for walks on the hill above the house
or dived for coins in the public pool
travelling together through the language
hand in hand
had we made it to Le Cigne
as we made it to the Shelly Banks

Age and drink dimmed that for us
still there was a moment there
I almost had us in a frame together
cycling through sunflowers down the Liffey Quays
that time you from the crowd
played stand-in for a missing goalie
in the Phoenix Park
forty years ago —
or dying for Ireland on the stage in Dublin
or checking your football pools in Sandymount
hopefully
on Sundays before the pubs opened
or hunting amethysts above Keem Bay for therapy

I remember this
middle-aged on these Italian steps
and understand the down-turn of your mouth
under siege and quizzical
echoed in my own
wondering how in the end we got here

Niall plays in the sunny yard below
I bequeath him summer and these sunflowers